Daddy's Waiting On You...

By

Rickey E. Macklin

authorHOUSE

1663 LIBERTY DRIVE, SUITE 200
BLOOMINGTON, INDIANA 47403
(800) 839-8640
www.authorhouse.com

© 2004 Rickey E. Macklin
All Rights Reserved.

No part of this book may be reproduced, stored in a retrieval system, or transmitted by any means without the written permission of the author.

First published by AuthorHouse 05/24/04

ISBN: 1-4184-2108-1 (e)
ISBN: 1-4184-2107-3 (sc)

Printed in the United States of America
Bloomington, Indiana

This book is printed on acid-free paper.

"AND THERE I WILL MEET WITH THEE, AND I WILL COMMUNE WITH THEE FROM ABOVE THE MERCY SEAT, FROM BETWEEN THE TWO CHERUBIMS WHICH ARE UPON THE ARK OF THE TESTIMONY, OF ALL THINGS WHICH I WILL GIVE THEE IN COMMANDMENT UNTO THE CHILDREN OF ISRAEL."

EXODUS 25:22

"AND THE LORD SPAKE UNTO MOSES FACE TO FACE, AS A MAN SPEAKETH UNTO HIS FRIEND."

EXODUS 33:11

Rickey E. Macklin

Foreword by
Elder Mom Edith Faulk Joynes

This book was written to assist the believer in discovering a relationship with God beyond the vail.

SPECIAL THANKS

To my parents, Reverend Arthur C. Macklin Sr. and Maria W. Macklin, who intercede for me constantly

To all ten of my siblings – Earl, Sylvia, Arthur Jr., Otis, Gazella, Rogina, Teresa, Towanna, Angel and Crystal

To my Ambassadors For Christ family

To Tommy Tenney and his Spirit-Inspired masterpiece "God Chasers"

And to my Jericho City of Praise family

THANK YOU ALL

DEDICATION

This Book is

Dedicated

to

the Glory of

THE LORD JESUS CHRIST

Who through the Eternal Spirit has imparted unto me divine enlightenment on the matter of divine intimacy.

Special Thanks

To All of those who have taken the time to develop intimacy with Daddy and have passed on your experience with so many others.

TABLE OF CONTENTS

SPECIAL THANKS vii
DEDICATION ix
FOREWORD xiii
INTRODUCTION: xv
CHAPTER ONE: TEARS OF JOY 1
CHAPTER TWO: PURSUING INTIMACY WITH DADDY 9
CHAPTER THREE: WHY I CALL HIM DADDY 19
CHAPTER FOUR: ESTABLISHING INTIMACY WITH DADDY 27
   OUTER COURT – INNNER COURT – HOLIEST OF HOLIES EXPERIENCE 28
   OUT OF EGYPT – THROUGH THE WILDERNESS – INTO THE PROMISE LAND 36
   THE CHRISTIAN WALK FROM BABYHOOD – TO ADOLESCENCE – TO MATURATION IN CHRIST 42
CHAPTER FIVE: SHOW ME YOUR GLORY 59
CHAPTER SIX: MAINTAINING INTIMACY WITH DADDY 63
CONCLUSION: COME CLOSER… 71
SCRIPTURES TO ASSIST YOU IN YOUR JOURNEY BEYOND THE VAIL 74
REFERENCES 77

FOREWORD

The readers of this book, entitled "Daddy's Waiting On You" written by Minister Rickey E. Macklin, will be blessed as it reveals that it is absolutely imperative for all believers to develop a relationship of intimacy "beyond the vail." There the grace and mercy of the Trinity brought about by the life, death, burial and resurrection of our Lord and Savior Jesus Christ grants us permission to enter into the Holy of Holies. (Hebrews 9)

This book shares the process involved in getting believers to the place where God can constantly tabernacle with us as we become "His" dwelling place.

(Psalms 91)

So get ready to:
- **Release** your tears of joy
- **Pursue** your intimacy with Daddy
- **Establish** your intimacy with Daddy
- **Maintain** your intimacy with Daddy

"Daddy's Waiting On You" contains a message that believers will not only read and share with others, but also will become doers themselves of the message penned. (James 1:22)

Elder Mom Edith Faulk Joynes
Jericho City of Praise Ministries

INTRODUCTION:

Of all the wonderful things that can be done or acquired in this life, nothing is more satisfying than time alone with Daddy-God beyond the vail. Yet, the reality of life somehow still brings all of us to numerous questions. What am I going to do in life? Where am I going next? Should I take this job? What's my purpose? What school should I attend? Who am I to marry? Did I marry the right person? Should I buy a house now or should I wait? When should I start pastoring? Should I have children? What about my career? If I questioned you, I'm sure you could include an additional five questions to this list. We've equally had our share of answering these questions. As a result, there have been many divorces, failed churches, abortions, foreclosures, frustrated employees and neglected children. I'm often reminded of Psalm 127:1, 2.

> *1. Except the Lord build the house, they labour in vain that build it: except the Lord keep the city, the watchman waketh but in vain.*
> *2. It is vain for you to rise up early, to sit up late, to eat the bread of sorrows: for so he giveth his beloved sleep.*

As I look at the above passage, I am reminded of the divine favor of God. It is clear to me in this passage that if the Lord is not the builder of the house, or as Pastor Betty Peebles would say, *"If the Lord does not provide the blueprint,"* then all the laboring that you do and all the sweat you put into it is simply in vain. What is the house? Well, it could be your family, your job, the selection of your mate or even the purpose *you* choose rather than God's purpose you discover. In other words, you cannot go off and do things your own way and then expect for God to come and bless them. No! Just find out God's plan and purpose and the blessings and favor of God will already be in it and upon it! The next part of the scripture says, *"except the Lord keep the city, the watchmen waketh but in vain."* What are you saying here, David? It's sort of like this – You can be as alert as possible in the natural but if you haven't tapped into the spiritual realm to see what Daddy has to say, the enemy will still come in – spoil your goods and destroy your home. Why? Because the Lord didn't give you the blueprint, therefore, the Lord is not obligated to keep it. Verse two says, *"It is vain for you to rise up early, to sit up late, to eat the bread of sorrows: for so he giveth his beloved sleep."* Nice finishing touch. God says it is useless. You are wasting your time getting up early, going to bed late, eating the bread of sorrow and worrying about something that you can't fix. If you had gotten God's plan from the beginning, you would understand that God gives his beloved sleep and you could truly – *go to bed.*

In this book, the Holy Spirit will indeed lead you to that place of absolute rest in God. Sure there are many questions, but there are also many answers. Although we have these questions, just for a moment, let's lay them aside and see what Daddy is waiting on. There is a place reserved just for you on the other side of the mountain. A place where you can climb up on Daddy's lap, lay your head on His chest, and have an experience with Him that will change your life forever! I've been blessed with the experience and have returned to let you know that *Daddy is now waiting on you.*

CHAPTER ONE

TEARS OF JOY

TEARS OF JOY

My heart and mind were set on finding out, who was my mate? What was God's next move for my life? How long would it take? And where was He taking me in ministry? I had so many unanswered questions and I was about to set out on a venture to find out the answer to every one. For these answers, the Holy Spirit led me on a forty day fast. At this point in my life, there were so many distractions until I could not imagine getting these answers any other way. However, as I began this forty day fast, I did not understand that my greatest reason for fasting would turn out to be reuniting with Him. Somehow in the process of doing the work of the Lord, I lost contact with the Lord of the work. I was so excited, thrilled and literally ecstatic about this fast because I knew that I would get all of my answers. Some time ago, I had learned that how bad you want something would be determined by what you were willing to give up. To me, this was an extreme situation and it required an extreme sacrifice but I was determined to give up everything. On day three, however, something eye-wakening yet painful occurred. It became very evident that my affection for God had deteriorated. I was talking to a very dear friend of mine and midway in the conversation my heart became heavy. I believe it was the heaviest it had been since coming into the body of Christ. I said to her, "I don't love Him anymore." What was I basing this on? I'm sure that everyone reading this book can identify with love in one way or another and if not love, at least the emotions associated with it. There was a time that when I thought of Him, my heart would go pitter-patter. The mushy feelings would come and I would get lost somewhere in the glory. Even in corporate and personal worship, I would find myself lying prostrate before Him in tears. But at this point of my life, there was no lying out before Him nor were there any more tears. I didn't have the mushy feelings and I was not going to attempt to conjure them up. They simply were not there. At this point, I was only going through the motions. I said to my friend again - "I don't love Him anymore."

Needless to say, I went through a battle within for the next three days. I literally felt like the church of Ephesus that Jesus scrutinized in the book of Revelation. Jesus said to her, out of all the good works you do, and your labor, and your patience, and how you can't even deal with those folks that are evil: I still have something recorded against you, Ephesus. You have left your first love. (Revelation 2:2-4)

AT THIS POINT, I WAS ONLY GOING THROUGH THE MOTIONS. I SAID TO MY FRIEND AGAIN – "I DON'T LOVE HIM ANYMORE."

I cannot begin to tell you how bad I felt and neither am I going to try. Had I really left my first love? How could I have drifted so far away from Him? How did I allow my public praise and worship to replace my private intimate time with Him? However, on day seven, to my delight, by the grace and mercy of God, I had another conversation with my friend and in the midst of talking about Him, every emotion and every feeling that I had ever experienced seemed to have flooded my heart. As I continued to talk, the tears began to flow. I said to her – "I do love Him - I really do love Him!" My friend, I must be honest with you. All those questions that I had going into the fast became completely absorbed in reestablishing intimacy with Daddy. None of them mattered anymore. I began to inquire of Him as to how to create a constant flow of communion and He revealed it as plain as day. At this point, I realized that He desired this intimacy with me long before I came to desire it with Him. In essence, He was waiting on me!

My instructions were to meet Him every evening. As a husband would romance his wife, God wanted me to romance Him. I was to create the atmosphere for love. In the natural, a husband would start the day off with wonderful words of intimacy. Around noonday, he would call his wife, not for a long conversation but just to let her know that she was on his mind. He would then close the conversation with an expression of his love for her in anticipation of seeing her later. Upon arriving home, he would greet her with a kiss and flowers. Perhaps he would cook her favorite meal; run her bath water at the prescribed temperature; put a slow song on; turn the lights down low; then whisper sweet words in her ear… Hey, I believe that God allows us to experience some things in the natural so that we can at least have an idea of how to approach Him in the spirit. With a wife or a husband, the benefits are wonderful but limited. With God, the benefits are out of this world. Wow! What an experience! What did I do? I followed this same pattern in the spirit. From sweet words of intimacy in the morning - affirming my love to Him at noonday - to meeting Him at night. I bought every worship CD and one specific DVD I found that I knew would create the right atmosphere to take me into His presence. I listened to the CD's at work and watched the DVD at night with Him. I eliminated everything I knew of in my life that could keep me from this experience. There wasn't a night that I fell asleep that wasn't preceded with tears. Every night before going to bed I would

Daddy's Waiting On You...

tell Him how much I loved Him and then I would thank Him for rekindling the fire. Every night - and I'm not exaggerating, I felt as though it was the arms of God wrapping me securely in His bosom rocking me to sleep. For the first time in years, I recognized my true need for Him. Every breath that I breathed became totally dependent on Him. My original questions changed to - What was I going to do? Where was I going to go? How was I supposed to function? Without a word from Him, I was lost. As babies are dependent on their parents, I was likewise dependent on Him. I felt so helpless and inadequate in His presence. I truly needed Him - not for a mate or a job or even ministry. I needed Him for my very existence. At this point, I didn't care if any of those questions were ever answered. I simply could hardly wait for the next night of intimacy with Daddy.

As I continued on with the fast, our line of communication became more and more clear. He then revealed to me that He desired these same kinds of experiences with His other children as well. At least three times after that word, He had me specifically talk to certain individuals. I told them of my time with Him and how it was as if I were basking in the lilies of the field on the other side of the mountain. I told them that it was as if He had sent me back to let them know that "Daddy was waiting on them."

So, what was the culmination of this experience? This was all leading up to the last day of the fast. I was to speak at a retreat for the Singles Ministry of a local church. And get this – it was in the mountains – GLORY! I knew that something was going to happen. The word that the Lord had given me was, "I Don't Want A Part-time Lover!" My God! In 1 Kings chapter 18, the Prophet Elijah first told the people to decide whom they would serve. This was of course a result of King Ahab's marriage to Jezebel (A Phoenician Princess) for political alliances. As a result of this compromise, God literally shut up the heavens for three and a half years. If you were to ask me, I would tell you that the greatest problem here was not the absence of rain but it was the absence of the presence of God. Secondly, the Prophet Elijah placed the sacrifice on the altar. God's fire doesn't fall without a sacrifice. Thirdly, the fire fell and consumed the sacrifice. Lastly, the Prophet Elijah constructed himself another altar, fell down with his face between his knees and called on God to send the rain. Oh My God! On my way driving up into the mountains, I saw fire. I said, yes Lord! As I kept driving, I saw the water flowing. I said, yes Lord! And as I continued to drive, I saw the glory cloud surrounding the mountain. I said, have your way Lord! It was confirmed in my spirit. God was getting ready to do something phenomenal in that place. When I arrived, the praise team was in the middle of worship, and I knew without a doubt that He was already in the room and was about to forever change people's lives. By the end of the message, I had never seen people so desperate for an encounter with God. They were determined not to allow the moment to pass. Since Daddy was in the room, they were determined to get His attention. They put their sacrifices on the altar; the fire fell and consumed it; and the glory of God filled the room. There wasn't a dry eye in the room. We were all laid out before the Lord. Some on their knees, while the majority of us were on our faces crying and weeping before the Lord.

One last testimony, if you don't mind. Some five or six years ago I attended a small multi-cultural church in Washington, D.C. I had invested a lot of time in worship with Daddy, but little did I know that this night would be different from all others. As the praise team began to serenade Him with the sweet songs of worship, I joined in. Many times people have asked me what do I see or experience in my worship. Often times I see myself bowing down before His feet. There is a space in front of Him clearly marked off which no one enters, not even the angels, but on both sides of that space there seems to be constant worship. That's where I would end up every time I went into worship. He would be sitting upon His throne, and although I never saw His face, I knew it was Him. So, let us get back to the testimony. In that church I had an unforgettable experience. As Paul stated, "...*(whether in the body, I cannot tell; or whether out of the body, I cannot tell: God knoweth;) such as one caught up to the third heaven* (2 Corinthians 12:2)." It was beyond describing. The atmosphere was charged with glory and the sound… the sound – a sound such as I have never heard before in my life. The angels were singing unto Him. Then I turned towards the throne and saw Him, although I could not really see Him. It was more of a silhouette. I said to Him, "If this is what heaven is like, I don't want to leave." Dear one, you could have told all my family members that I wasn't coming back and I would have been fine with it. But He spoke to me and said one word at first. He said, PURPOSE. He went on to say, your purpose is not complete. Instantly, I found myself back in that church and as you might have already guessed, I was sobbing.

What an experience! Since that day, I have not been remiss of telling people the necessity in apprehending their God-given purposes. I don't know what it is about being close to God that produces tears. I heard one preacher say years ago that you can be emotional without being spiritual, but it's almost impossible to be spiritual without being emotional. My tears were tears of joy – the kind of joy that can only be experienced in His presence.

Rickey E. Macklin

CHAPTER TWO

PURSUING INTIMACY WITH DADDY

Rickey E. Macklin

PURSUING INTIMACY

Can the Creator of the universe really be known in an intimate way? What crosses your mind when you hear the term intimacy? I asked that question because I don't know if you're saved or unsaved or whether you are a babe or mature in Christ. What I am sure of is that people identify with the term in many different ways. For some, there are thoughts of holding hands, kissing and hugging. For others, thoughts of having sex come to mind. In the natural sense, if you are intimate with a man or a woman, the woman can give birth to a baby, both inheriting a responsibility that they may not have wanted at that time. However, in the spiritual sense, there is a far greater blessing in being intimate with God. Those that are intimate with Him are used to give birth to nations (those that will become sons of God, bearing His character and nature). They are the ones that receive greater insight, anointing and revelation.

Now, having said that, in the old Hebrew text, the writers not only honored Him but even His name was considered holy and to be protected. Yet you've heard me refer to Him on several occasions as Daddy. Does this diminish His holiness? Not at all. Am I using His name in vain? No. In this chapter, we will deal with two of His characteristics and somehow, through the help of the Holy Spirit, establish a balance between Creator and Daddy. You will discover that pursuing Him is not a bad idea after all.

One of the things that has troubled me for some time now has been the way we handle Him. I grew up in a generation in which the church building and the church ground were considered holy.

We felt that if you told a lie on the church ground, God would send lightening down from heaven and strike you. There was such a reverential fear for Him. However, many of us only knew Him as God. No communion. No fellowship. I had never heard of being intimate with God. I thought that being close to Him meant the Spirit would hit you and you would scream or cry, roll around on the floor, jump pews, jerk a few times or speak in tongues. Don't get me wrong, I'm not minimizing, making fun of or disrespecting those experiences, but there was so much more I needed to know. I never knew that the Holy Spirit was a *person* and not an it. While Jesus was giving some of His final words to His disciples, He spoke of the Holy Spirit by saying, *"But when the **Comforter** is come, whom I will send unto you from the Father, even the **Spirit of truth**, which proceedeth from the Father, **he** shall testify of me."* But in spite of a lack of knowledge, we feared God! As for the generation we live in now, I'm almost afraid. God is seen as "The Man Upstairs", and Jesus Christ is spoken of as "JC" who is looking out for me. Imagine trying to bind demons in the name of "JC." I'm sure that if the seven sons of Sceva were around today they would tell you, "don't even try it." (Acts 19:13-16) Someone may say to me – Well, Minister Rickey, don't you think that you are taking it a little too far? Quite frankly, I don't think so and neither does Jesus. In Matthew chapter six in the Lord's Prayer, Jesus says when you address the Father in prayer, begin your prayer by acknowledging how hollowed His name is. In other words, Your name is sacred – it's holy – it's to be respected, revered and honored. So no, I'm not taking it too far. Perhaps you're not taking it far enough. We've reached a time now where teenagers are having sex in the church. Church officials are living double lives (i.e., hypocrites), while many pastors are pimping and manipulating the body of Christ. Habakkuk cried out in a crisis like this and said to God, "How

Long?" After God showed Habakkuk the impending judgment to come, the word of the Lord says that his belly trembled and his lips quivered at the voice of God (Habakkuk 3:16). You see, many have taken advantage of the grace of God and unknowingly minimized Him to a created being. We've desecrated the house of God through vain philosophies. And whenever your view of God becomes distorted, your worship will too. Hence your lifestyle will portray that of someone who doesn't even know Him. (i.e., a heathen) Can a bridge be established between the two extremes? In actuality, it already has. Jesus bridged this gap almost 2,000 years ago. But before getting into that, let's talk about two of His characteristics.

AND WHENEVER YOUR VIEW OF GOD BECOMES DISTORTED, YOUR WORSHIP WILL TOO.

His Transcendence

The term transcendent means above and beyond; the superlative; independent of the material universe. It means that He is separate from and independent of the things He created. It also means that He is superior to them. He's detached insofar as His existence as God is concerned and superior insofar as being its Creator. He transcends man in knowledge, wisdom, power, love, goodness, holiness and purity. Don't ever make the mistake of putting yourself on the same playing field as God. Let's see what Isaiah says in the 40th chapter.

Verses 12-17,18,21-23,25,28

12. Who hath measured the waters in the hollow of his hand, and meted out heaven with the span, and comprehended the dust of the earth in a measure, and weighed the mountains in scales, and the hills in a balance?

13. Who hath directed the spirit of the Lord, or being his counseller hath taught him?

14. With whom took he counsel, and who instructed him, and taught him in the path of judgment, and taught him knowledge, and shewed to him the way of understanding?

15. Behold, the nations are as a drop of a bucket, and are counted as the small dust of the balance: behold, he taketh up the isles as a very little thing.

17. All nations before him are as nothing; and they are counted to him less than nothing, and vanity.

18. To whom then will ye liken God? or what likeness will ye compare unto him?

21. Have ye not known? have ye not heard? hath it not been told you from the beginning? have ye not understood from the foundations of the earth?

22. It is he that sitteth upon the circle of the earth, and the inhabitants thereof are as grasshoppers; that stretcheth out the heavens as a curtain, and spreadeth them out as a tent to dwell in:

23. That bringeth the princes to nothing; he maketh the judges of the earth as vanity.

25. <u>To whom then will ye liken me, or shall I be equal? saith the Holy One</u>.

28. Hast thou not known? hast thou not heard, that the everlasting God, the Lord, the Creator of the ends of the earth, fainteth not, neither is weary? there is no searching of his understanding.

So, as the older folks would say, "Child, don't you play with God." They were right. After viewing Him in this way, who would? As I reflect back over my own life and consider the times that I've completely disregarded His holiness and His omnipotence, I can only imagine where I would be if it were not for His grace.

His Immanence

The term immanent means existing or remaining within. In other words, even though He does not need us to exist – we need Him. Therefore, He is present and active within His creation. He's not as one William Paley called Him, "The Great Clock Maker." The One who created the universe and like a clock wound it up and let it go. No! The word of God says, *"He upholds all things by the word of His power."* (Heb 1:3) Job said, *"All the while my breath is in me, and the spirit of God is in my nostrils."* (27:3) Then in the book of Acts, the Apostle Paul says, *"For in him we live, and move, and have our being..."* (17:28) We do not have the ability to operate independent of God.

Now, having said all of that, this transcendent God wants to be known intimately by His people. However, the tendency to emphasize one or the other will lead to a faulty conception of God. I understand the predicament. Many children have become confused and have faulty conceptions of their parents. I'm sure that many parents would love to establish friendships with their children. I don't know very many parents who would not love for their children to share personal things that they are going through in their lives. The dilemma is creating that kind of atmosphere without it going too far. What's too far? It's when they begin to talk to you like a peer; address you like a peer; treat you like a peer and do things around you that they only do around their peers. For instance, I've met parents who think that it is okay for their children to perform certain unbiblical acts in their homes. The justification is they would much rather allow them to do it at home than somewhere in the streets where no one really cares about them. So, they drink together, smoke together, and are allowed to take sexual partners to their bedrooms. Oh, while I have yet to mention it, they also fuss, cuss and fight together. I don't think this is too difficult for you to grasp since all respect is probably lost at this time. Do these parents not know that God is holding them responsible? They will one day stand before Him and give an account for their stewardship. As a result of this, many parents refuse to establish friendships with their children because the relationship can easily become misconstrued. God, on the other hand, doesn't have this problem. In this, He reaches out to us and calls us friends.

Now, it's important that you understand what a friend is before you go too far. Webster's Dictionary defines a friend as a person whom ones knows, likes and trusts. Furthermore, it's a person with whom one is allied in a struggle or cause. In my words, a friend is someone who understands you and puts up with you in spite of you. It is someone with whom you can trust to come through for you when no one else can or will. They pledge their loyalty to you in the good times and bad times. Note that this is not just someone to hang out and have fun with. You can do that with anyone. This person is dependable and honest with you even if it hurts. As a friend, God has pledged to be allied with us even in our trouble and to deliver us with honor. (Psalms 91:15) It is our duty to maintain the balance between this Holy God and Friend. Although God is present when we need Him, we should still be in awe in regards to His sovereignty. You would be appalled to know how distorted some Christian's views are of Him. Although God is your friend, He is not Sonya, Sally Sue, Mike or Renee. He's not your boy that you kick it with or your girl that you sit around the table and have frivolous conversations with. First of all, God does not waste words. Every word spoken by Him is full of power and is unalterable. Whatever He says comes into being. Can you imagine Him saying, "Girl, you're crazy?" You may as well give out your new address {mental institution}. You can't invite or invoke His presence and then talk to Him any kind of way. He is not looking to be entertained.

Furthermore, although He wants to be known intimately, please don't confuse that with sensuality. Other gods required all types of sexual and illicit acts to appease them. As for God, He may be the lover of your soul but your body was created for His glory in order to assist the mandate on your spirit. That's why we should take care of it but not worship it. Even with the term Daddy, as endearing and intimate as it is, there is also an established level of respect and dependence. Just remember that He's holy and pure and don't you be found guilty of making Him a god of flesh. We must not deduce His Holiness through our humanistic perceptions and preconceptions. What are you saying Minister Rickey? You may have had the best dad in the world. As a result of this, your conception of daddy is good but it still does not compare to God. Or you may have had a dad at home but didn't show you any love, affection or fulfilled any of his headship responsibilities. Your concept may be that of a weak and non-affectionate dad. Or perhaps you may have had a dad that pops up every now and then. Your conception of him may be non-dependable, irresponsible and slack. On the other hand, you may not have ever seen your dad before in your life and perhaps its because he disowned you. Your concept may be full of rejection and bitterness. Through life experiences, one way or another, we draw conclusions based on our past. We perceive Daddy-God to be what our pasts have taught us. I simply want to tell you today my sisters and my brothers – allow God to erase your past. What God wants to show you about a real Dad will change your life forever. Now, having said all of that, God knows that to know Him is to love Him. Knowing Him implies that you've invested time with Him. You've gotten to know Him through intimacy. Here are a few scriptures on knowing Him.

> *Jeremiah 9:23-24*
> *23. Thus saith the Lord, Let not the wise man glory in his wisdom, neither let the mighty man glory in his might, let not the rich man glory in his riches:*
> *24. But let him that glorieth glory in this, that he understandeth and **knoweth me**, that I am the Lord which exercise lovingkindness, judgment, and righteousness, in the earth: for in these things I delight, saith the Lord.*

Here's another…

> *John 17:3*
> *And this is life eternal, **that they might know thee the only true God**, and Jesus Christ, whom thou hast sent.*

And another…

> *I John 5:20*
> *And we know that the Son of God is come, and hath given us an understanding, **that we may know him that is true, and we are in him that is true, even in his Son Jesus Christ**. **This is the true God, and eternal life**.*

Moses says,

> *Deuteronomy 33:13*
> *Teach me your ways, **so that I may know you**, and continue to find favor with You.*

John finishes it off by saying that not only does God want to be known but He is known by His children ...

> *I John 2:13*
> *I write unto you, fathers, because ye have known him that is from the beginning. I write unto you, young men, because ye have overcome the wicked one. **I write unto you, little children, because ye have known the Father**.*

Prayer:

Father, give me a heart to know You and to know your son Lord Jesus Christ in the power of his resurrection and the fellowship of his suffering. Cause me to know the abiding presence of your Holy Spirit who lives within me.

Thank You, Daddy

CHAPTER THREE
WHY I CALL HIM DADDY

Why I Call Him Daddy

So, what about the term Daddy, and why do I call Him that? The reason why is because it's a very affectionate, intimate and endearing term. Daddy is really an informal way of saying father. The term father means covering, provider, sustainer, cultivator, originator, source and keeper. Webster's Encyclopedic Unabridged Dictionary defines fatherly as paternal – referring to the relationship of a male to his children. It has emotional connotations; it always suggests a kind, protective, tender, or forbearing attitude. As I stated in the previous chapter, this concept may be rather difficult for those of you who do not have or have never experienced a real father. This may have left you feeling fragmented, but your spiritual Dad has and will always be there. For those of you who have, I'm sure that you can say of your own father that he's someone that loves you; affirms you; cares affectionately for you; he's dependable; supplying all your needs; does whatever is necessary to make sure you're happy; and gives you sound advice. I call Him Daddy because He is all those things to me.

So, how do we establish this same kind of relationship with the Father of the universe? Here are some ingredients that are going to be required.

- Investing Time
- Studying His word
- Meditation upon the word
- Prayer
- Praise & Worship
- Fasting

A) *Invest some time getting to know Him.* Don't rush the moments. Take full advantage of every opportunity you get to hang around Him. Oh, did I mention, with no strings attached? In other words, you are not hanging out with Him because of what He can do for you. As Tommy Tenny stated in God Chasers, "God said to stop seeking His hand and to seek His face." As with any matured relationship in the natural, time is essential. So it is in the spiritual realm. Some things simply take time. Time to cultivate and time to grow. But when it has become matured, ten minutes away from Him feels like an eternity. (Psalms 27:4)

B) *Studying His word.* Well, in order to meditate on the above, you are going to have to study. 2 Timothy 2:15 says, *"Study to shew thyself approved unto God, a workman that needeth not to be ashamed, rightly dividing the word of truth."* In other words, study like you're in the gym working out. And just remember that you are doing it to be approved of God not man. Man doesn't have a heaven or a hell to put you in.

C) *Meditate upon His word and Him.* Meditate on His goodness, His mercy, His longsuffering, His kindness, His attributes, His principles and His promises. At some point, you'll find yourself on the subway train thinking about Him. You'll find that the long ride home from work, no longer seems long enough. At school, you're thinking of Him. When in conversations that literally have nothing to do with Him, somehow you find yourself gravitating to one word that reminds you of how wonderful Daddy is. (Joshua 1:8)

D) *Prayer.* In prayer we covey our feelings to Daddy and He coveys His will to us. A songwriter once wrote that "prayer is the key to the kingdom and faith unlocks the door." To me, prayer is awesome in that it establishes a medium of communication with someone who is greater than you. With this medium we can communicate our thanksgiving, praise, worship, petitions, acknowledgement of our sins and receive forgiveness. Think of it like this. When you approach your earthly daddy with adoration and thanksgiving, although you may not have expressed your next need to him, he oftentimes foresees it and grants it anyway. When we pray, the grace and power of God is transmitted to us to enable us to be more than conquerors. The bottom line is there are some things that neither you, your momma, your earthly daddy nor your mate can do. James R. Peebles, Sr. once stated, "More Prayer, More Power." In other words, a praying man or woman of God is a force to be reckoned with. (James 5:16)

E) *Praise & Worship.* When we praise God, we are telling Him that based upon His character we trust Him. Regardless of what's going on in our lives, we magnify Him over and beyond it. When I look at my problems and what I'm going through and then turn and take a look at Him – my problem is not a problem after all. After praising, we progress into worship. If you praised Him all the time but never went into worship, you would be nothing more than a teaser. After pumping God up and setting the atmosphere, God wants intimacy. In worship, you yield yourself to the true and living God. It is the climax, the pinnacle, the apex, and the peak of our relationship with Him. The word of God says that the Father seeks worshippers that will do it in spirit and in truth. This scripture tells me that if the Father has to seek them then there must be a shortage. It is my belief that worship is a part of our nature. It's just the way He made us. The issue is who and what we worship. For some people it's their houses, cars, degrees and social economic status. For many others, it's their husbands, wives and children. So then, a worshipper is easy to find. God says the problem is finding a true worshipper. In worship, we make an exchange but receive the greater reward. (Matthew 21:16; John 4:23,24)

F) *Fasting.* Fasting doesn't change God but it does change us. One of the greatest benefits I've found in fasting is that it decreases the sensitivity of our flesh and increases the sensitivity of our spirits to the Spirit of God. When we fast two things are sure to happen – (1) sanctification {to set apart for sacred use} and (2) consecration {to declare as holy}. What's the connection with these twins? While sanctification sets us apart from the world and worldly habits, consecration is the process of dedicating and devoting oneself to the service of the Lord. I am aware that there are several reasons in the word of God to go on or to call a fast i.e., laying of hands for ministry; drawing close to God in times of trouble; handling difficult situations; loosening the bands of wickedness; undoing heavy burdens; releasing the oppress; and destroying every yoke of the enemy. However, knowing that it's going to bring me to a closer walk with Him out-weighs them all. Fasting should be a normal part of a Christian's walk. (2 Corinthians 6:17; Romans 6:13; Exodus 28:3)

WHILE SACTIFICATION SETS US APART FROM THE WORLD AND WORLDLY HABBITS, CONSECRATION IS THE PROCESS OF DEDICATING AND DEVOTING ONESELF TO THE SERVICE OF THE LORD.

Here are a few more scriptures for your meditation.

David's testimony...

Psalm 42:1-2
1. As the hart (deer) panteth after the water brooks, so panteth my soul after thee, O God.

2. My soul thirsteth for God, for the living God: when shall I come and appear before God?

Psalm 27:4
One thing have I desired of the Lord, that will I seek after; that I may dwell in the house of the Lord all the days of my life, to behold the beauty of the Lord, and to inquire in his temple.

And finally, Paul's testimony...

Philippians 3:8-10
8. Yea doubtless, and I count all things but loss for the excellency of the knowledge of Christ Jesus my Lord: for whom I have suffered the loss of all things, and do count them but dung, that I may win Christ,
9. And be found in him, not having mine own righteousness, which is of the law, but that which is through the faith of Christ, the righteousness which is of God by faith:
*10. **That I may know him**, and the power of his resurrection, and the fellowship of his sufferings, being made conformable unto his death;*

In summation, whenever speaking of God and his characteristics, one cannot help but become overwhelmed by His Excellency! This God, our God, the only wise, true and living God has given us a peek into HIM. Yes, Jesus truly bridged this gap. In Jesus, God became Man yet never ceased from being God. As God, he remained sovereign, omnipotent, omniscient and omnipresent. But as Man, He was subjected to the very nature He created. As God, He received worship from man and angels but as Man, He was despised and rejected. He was indeed as the Hebrew writer states, "touched with the feelings of our infirmities." My God! But it was necessary. The word of God says that we were alienated, lost without God and had no hope in this world. But then Jesus superimposed limitations upon himself to pay a price that could not be paid any other way. We were at odds with Him, and the only agent that was designed to bring reconciliation with the Father was the blood of Jesus. Jesus died to do for us what we could never do for ourselves. As a result thereof, the middle wall of partition that separated us from Him for so many years was ripped apart. Now, because He has chosen to reveal Himself to us, we are not like others who worship their strange, unknowable and created gods. (Phil 2:6-8; Eph 2:12-16; Hebrews 10:11,12) When I think of Him and of who He really is; of His divine nature and the intimacy I get to experience with Him; the fact that the God of the universe allows me to call Him Daddy, I am left perplexed and bewildered. Yes, I am left only with one question in mind, "Who wouldn't serve a God like this?"

CHAPTER FOUR

ESTABLISHING INTIMACY WITH DADDY

OUTER COURT – INNNER COURT – HOLIEST OF HOLIES EXPERIENCE

One of the biggest problems one can make is to involve oneself in a relationship with another, when one has not established an intimate relationship with God first. The reason why is because He is love and until you fall in love with Him, you will never be capable of truly loving another. Only He can truly teach you how to love His sons and daughters. Now, since Daddy is indeed waiting on us, let's do our best to get to the place where we can constantly experience what He has for us. In this chapter, we will cover three diagrams; (1) The Tabernacle of Moses; (2) The Voyage of Israel from Egypt to the Promise Land; and (3) The Christian progressive walk from babyhood to maturity in Christ.

The tabernacle was a portable sanctuary for the Israelites. It was also commonly referred to as the tent of meeting. Simply put – it was a primary place where God met with His people. In Exodus 25, God gave Moses specific instructions on how this tabernacle was to be constructed. I believe the one scripture I love the most in the entire chapter is verse twenty-two. God said to Moses, *"And there I will meet with thee, and I will commune with thee from above the mercy seat, from between the two cherubims which are upon the ark of the testimony, of all things which I will give thee in commandment unto the children of Israel."* God's place of communion has always been established. He met with Moses beyond the vail, and that's where he will meet you and me.

The Outer Court of the tabernacle was a place of all man things – a place of carnality – a place of flesh. But it was also a place of thanksgiving. In Psalms 100:4 David said, *"Enter into his gates with thanksgiving, and into his courts with praise: be thankful unto him, and bless his name."* When a person entered the gates, they were entering the Outer Court area. But when they went into the Inner Court, they would be entering the Holy Place. God is saying thanksgiving is required in the Outer Court, but Praise is required in the Holy Place. Did they have anything to thank God for? Sure, for His sustaining power, for His provisions and for His deliverance out of Egypt.

The first step of progression in the Outer Court was the brazen alter. It was the place of sacrifice. What is a sacrifice? Webster's University Dictionary defines it as to forfeit (one thing) for another thing thought to be of greater value. In other words, you do not make a real sacrifice for something that you consider less than the value of what you are sacrificing. As a matter of fact, the act itself is not consistent with the definition of sacrifice. So then when you make a sacrifice, you are doing it by virtue of the fact that something greater is coming. Now what's amazing about a sacrifice to God is that not only does that which you are sacrificing mean a lot to you, but it also means a lot to God. What are you talking about, Minister Rickey? Here's what I'm saying. That thing, whatever it is - bulls, goats, heifers (job, degrees, relationships) that you hold fast to; that you deem to have sustained you to some degree – could be the very same thing that you will have to take a knife to in order to have an experience with God. Why is it important to God? Because He knows that a transfer is necessary. He cannot give you what He has for you until you give Him what He knows is not the best for you. If you recall in Genesis chapter 22:1-18, God commanded Abraham to place Isaac, his only son, on the altar as a sacrifice. Even though

Abraham had received a word from God that He was going to use Isaac as a conduit for the many generations to come, Abraham still obeyed God. Abraham's simple act of obedience was all God really wanted. In the end, God spared Isaac's life and provided a substitute sacrifice instead. As for the Priest, his job was to kill the sacrifice on the brazen alter. After having completed this task, blood would be everywhere.

HE CANNOT GIVE YOU WHAT HE HAS FOR YOU UNTIL YOU GIVE HIM WHAT HE KNOWS IS NOT THE BEST FOR YOU.

He was also required to gather some of that blood from the sacrifice because it would be needed later in the Most Holy Place (Holiest of All) to sprinkle over the Mercy Seat. The Priest would then proceed on to the Laver – the place of washing and cleansing. Surely you can see why this would be necessary, although symbolic in nature.

Onward, the Priest would go into the next area of the tabernacle – The Holy Place. This room had within it the lampstand with seven candles, the table of shewbread and the Bronze Altar, also known as the Altar of Incense. This room is also known as the Inner Court. When the Priest made it to this place, he was one stage past what God had done and a step closer to who He was. In the Outer Court you thank Him for His sacrificial works, but in the Inner Court you praise Him for who He is. As one songwriter puts it – "Just because He's God!" Here, there was a mixture of man and God things. There were the candles that represented humanity and the church. The oil that filled the lamp represented the Holy Spirit, but the priest had to dress the lamp daily and put oil in it. There was the table of shewbread, which represented Christ as provision and sustainer. Then there was the Altar of Incense. This was clearly symbolic of prayer, praise and worship of the saints going up as a sweet smelling savor in the nostrils of God. The priest would take the tongs and bring coals in from the brazen altar and place them on the Altar of Incense. He would then take the God-prescribed dosage of prepared four incenses and sprinkle it over the altar, producing an aroma that would slip its way through the vail and fill the Most Holy Place, producing a smile on the face of God. (Exodus 25-31)

> *Ex 30:34*
> *And the LORD said to Moses: Take sweet spices, stacte and onycha and galbanum, and pure frankincense with these sweet spices; there shall be equal amounts of each.*

This incense like the sacred anointing oil was considered so holy that the people were forbidden to copy it for personal use. Furthermore, the proper ingredients and the proper persons mixing them were so important until God said anyone attempting to do it any other way would suffer death at the hands of God Himself!

> *Leviticus 10:1-3*
> *1. And Nadab and Abihu, the sons of Aaron, took either of them his censer, and put fire therein, and put incense thereon, and offered strange fire before the Lord, which he commanded them not.*
> *2. And there went out fire from the Lord, and devoured them, and they died before the Lord.*

> *3. Then Moses said unto Aaron, This is it that the Lord spake, saying, I will be sanctified in them that come nigh me, and before all the people I will be glorified. And Aaron held his peace.*

Progressing onward, the high priest would enter the Most Holy Place. In the Outer Courts, he gave thanks; in the Inner Courts, he praised; but the Most Holy Place was a place of worship. This was a place of total submission and relinquishment to the Almighty God. There were no mixtures of man and God things in there. Beyond the vail in the Holy of Holies, it was purely God. But what was this vail that separated even the priests and the people from the Holy of Holies? The vail was a blue, purple, and scarlet curtain made with fine twined linen. (Exodus: 26:31-36) It was used to separate the Outer Court from the Holy Place and to separate the Holy Place from the Most Holy Place. The significance can really be traced back to the Garden of Eden. When Adam and Eve were exiled out of the garden, they were in essence being separated from God. Through the tabernacle and the vail, God was able to once again fellowship with man although in a limited status. Through the use of offerings, God temporarily covered the stench of the people's sins and allowed a selected priest to come into His presence once a year. There was however a two-fold problem associated with this process. The first problem was that the procedure had to be done all over again each year. The second and probably the greatest problem was that mankind was limited to fellowshipping with God through the representation of only one man. In other words, God was still separated from the rest of His people whom He loved so much. But as much as He loved them, He could not violate His holiness and commune with darkness. Can you imagine being in love with someone and not being able to see them? However, there could

Daddy's Waiting On You...

not be a coming together of righteousness and wretchedness, of the holy and the unholy, of the divine and the secular. On one side of the vail there was a Holy God and on the other sinful man. This is what the vail represented. As much as it hurt God to be separated from us, it was absolutely necessary.

We needed a permanent solution that would allow not just a priest but also each of us access beyond the vail; a solution that would satisfy God's desire and our need. What could remove that curtain that kept us at odds with Him for so long? It would take something great. The best offerings that man offered weren't good enough. What or who would be worthy of such a task? You'll find the answer in Genesis chapter 22 verses seven and eight. Isaac asked his father Abraham where was the burnt offering and his father replied with an answer I don't believe even he understood at that moment. It was an answer that would one day solve the sin problem once and for all.

> *7. And Isaac spake unto Abraham his father, and said, My father: and he said, Here am I, my son. And he said, Behold the fire and the wood: but where is the lamb for a burnt offering?*
> *8. And Abraham said, My son,* **God will provide himself a lamb for a burnt offering**: *so they went both of them together.*

God will provide Himself (JESUS) the Lamb for the burnt offering. It took God coming on the other side of the vail to solve the sin problem and satisfy God on the other side. How could a vail that God put in place separate God from Himself? When Jesus died on that old rugged cross, the bible says that the **vail of the temple was rent in two from the top to the bottom.**

(Matthew 27:50-52) What a day and what an hour. From the top to bottom, from heaven to earth, God sent a very clear message that a new and living way had been established. God's desire and our need could now be fulfilled. In the book of Ephesians 2: 13,14, the Apostle Paul says, *"But now in Christ Jesus ye who sometimes were far off are made nigh by the blood of Christ. For he is our peace, who hath made both one, and hath broken down the middle wall of partition between us."* The writer of Hebrews goes on to say, *"By a new and living way, which he hath consecrated for us, through the vail, that is to say, his flesh."* (Hebrews 10:20) What's the relevance and what's the significance? Jesus' torn and ripped body has allowed us access, a peek into him – the right to commune with Him. (GLORY!)

Now, back to the transition, into the Most Holy Place. The high priest went in once a year only on the Day of Atonement. He would go in and make atonement for his own sins and then offer sacrifice to atone for the sins of the people. He would receive a word of instruction from God and leave. There was no hanging around. In the Most Holy Place, there was only the Ark of the Covenant. The lid of the ark was called the mercy seat. It had upon it two gold cherubim (angels) that faced each other. However, in the ark were several things. It contained a gold pot filled with manna – again symbolic of God's sustaining power and provision (Exodus 16:33,34). There was Aaron's rod that budded – representing the authority, selection and election of God (Numbers 17:10). And finally, the tablets of the Ten Commandments – representing the word and will of God (Deuteronomy 10:4,5).

(See Ref A.1)

Daddy's Waiting On You...

The Tabernacle Of Moses

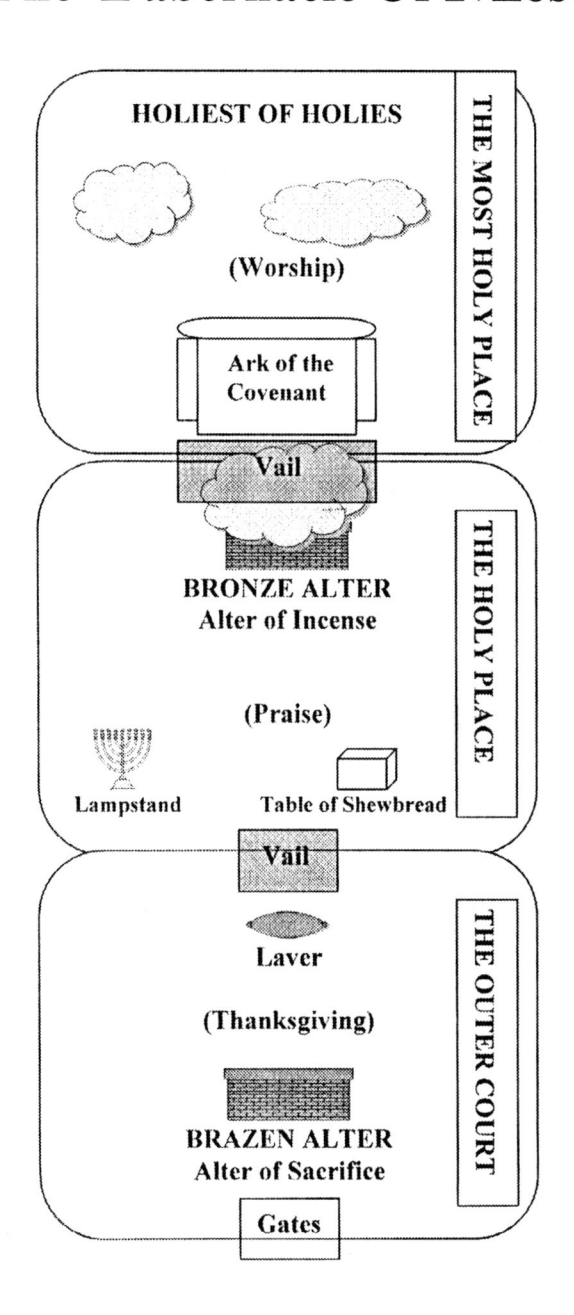

HOLIEST OF HOLIES

(Worship)

Ark of the Covenant

THE MOST HOLY PLACE

Vail

BRONZE ALTER
Alter of Incense

(Praise)

Lampstand   Table of Shewbread

THE HOLY PLACE

Vail

Laver

(Thanksgiving)

BRAZEN ALTER
Alter of Sacrifice

Gates

THE OUTER COURT

A.1

Rickey E. Macklin

OUT OF EGYPT – THROUGH THE WILDERNESS – INTO THE PROMISE LAND

In the book of Exodus, God raised Moses to be the deliverer for His people. Let me catch you up on the story in summary. The Moses story starts a few generations back with Joseph, the son of Jacob. Joseph was the first son of Jacob and Rachel and considered Jacob's favorite son. As a result of jealousy, Joseph's brothers sold him into slavery in Egypt. Joseph's tragedy eventually landed him in prison, but God was with him. (Genesis 39:20,21) His story carries him from the pit literally to the palace – second in command only to Pharaoh himself. Eventually, Joseph's entire family migrated to Egypt. Of course their stay in Egypt was by the divine purpose of God. Unfortunately, while in Egypt, two tragedies came upon God's people. One, after four hundred years, they lost contact with God and two, as the Pharaohs changed, the favor that Joseph had initially established was diminished. Israel was left without hope and without a friend. They were slaves making bricks out of straw… But God!

> *Exodus 2:23-25*
> *23. And it came to pass in process of time, that the king of Egypt died: and the children of Israel sighed by reason of the bondage, and they cried, and their cry came up unto God by reason of the bondage.*
> *24. And God heard their groaning, and God remembered his covenant with Abraham, with Isaac, and with Jacob.*
> *25. And God looked upon the children of Israel, and God had respect unto them.*

The word of God says, that He heard their cries and remembered His covenant with Abraham, with Isaac, and with Jacob. Notice that it wasn't because they had found pleasure in His sight, but it was because of God's covenant. This is important because each one of us came to God not of our own merits (our good works) but by the divine love of God. There is nothing you or I can do outside of Christ that could possibly please Him with the exception of saying, I yield – I yield. My Pastor preached a sermon years ago stating that everything you do outside of Christ that man considers good, are nothing more than mere good works *on the wrong side of the cross.*

THERE IS NOTHING YOU OR I CAN DO OUTSIDE OF CHRIST THAT COULD POSSIBLY PLEASE HIM WITH THE EXCEPTION OF SAYING,
I YIELD – I YIELD.

In other words, on heaven's calculator, it equates to vanity. Two things caught God's attention for Israel and these same two things will catch His attention for us. One, He heard their cries. Brokenness attracts Him. David said, *"The sacrifices of God are a broken spirit: a broken and a contrite heart, O God, thou wilt not despise.* (Psalm 51:17)" And two, His covenant. God's covenant is His word. His word is His bond. If He says a thing, it will surely come to pass. (Numbers 23:19,20) You see, although the Israelites didn't know Him, He knew them. And in maintaining His covenant, God raised Moses and established a relationship with him. Moses then became His mouthpiece. The potential problem that Moses faced was that although God had spoken with Him, He had not spoken to the people; therefore Moses was the only one to know the voice of God. To them, Moses was crazy, but to God, Moses was chosen. This would consequentially be the place of the rebirthing and reestablishment of His relationship with Israel.

In their messed-up degenerate state, God lifted them out of their bondage and miry clay, but it was still nothing more than an *Outer Court Relationship*. He then carried Israel, his bride, like a bridegroom into the bridal chamber – He carried her into the wilderness. There are several schools of thought about the wilderness, the length of time and why it was necessary. However, I'm going to scripturally tell you why the wilderness was necessary. In the book of Deuteronomy Chapter 8 verses two and three, the word of God makes it very plain.

> *Deuteronomy 8:2,3*
> *2. And thou shalt remember all the way which the Lord thy God led thee these forty years in the wilderness, to humble thee, and to prove thee, to know what was in thine heart, whether thou wouldest keep his commandments, or not.*
> *3. And he humbled thee, and suffered thee to hunger, and fed thee with manna, which thou knewest not, neither did thy fathers know; that he might make thee know that man doth not live by bread only, but by every word that proceedeth out of the mouth of the Lord doth man live.*

God says I have two reasons for your wilderness, Israel. The first reason is you need a humbling experience. When I get through with you, pride won't be an issue. When I take you into the Promised Land, you will know that you didn't get here on your own merits. You couldn't even deliver yourself out of Egypt – but I did! Why do I feel like I'm preaching to someone right now? Second reason – God says to Israel, I have to prove you. I have to try you like gold placed in the fire. In other words, after it has been all said and done, regardless of the extenuating circumstances, you will cling to what I have commanded of you. When I (God) bring you through, I have to know that I can trust you! It must be solidified. But in the wilderness, there were those who failed the test. The Bible says an entire generation died as a result of murmuring, complaining and disobedience. The wilderness can then be seen as a place of doubt, unbelief, complaint, deliverance from past, and a place of conflict. It can also, however, be seen as a place for supernatural interventions and manifestations of God. How were they to develop a real relationship with God and not a relationship based upon Moses' experience with Him? God would make provisions for this by revealing Himself to them. I may be of the old school mentality, but I still believe that in order to truly love someone, you first have to know him or her. So, how was God to be known? The word of God says that He suffered (allowed) them to become hungry. He allowed them to become thirsty. And when they could find no other resource to satisfy their needs, God stepped in and performed miracles. From manna sufficient for each day – to water gushing out of a rock – to a serpent of brass placed on a pole miraculously bringing healing. The Israelites came to know Him by covenant names like Jehovah-Rapha, Jehovah-Shalom, Jehovah-Nissi, Jehovah-Sabaoth and many, many others.

Eventually, the relationship was just right to go into Canaan, the land of promise. When Moses sent the twelve spies out to survey the land God promised them, we know from scripture that all but two came back with negative reports. Only Joshua and Caleb returned with words of faith. Because God had given them the land, they said we are well able to handle those giants. An important note is that although God brought them into this place, He did not rid the land of the enemy. Don't allow the enemy to deceive you into thinking that just because you are experiencing opposition you are not where God wants you to be. Sometimes the mere fact that you are experiencing opposition is proof that you are right where He wants you! Just know that He will make provisions and divinely protect you as with David in Psalms 23 verse 5.

> *- Thou preparest a table before me in the presence of mine enemies: thou anointest my head with oil; my cup runneth over. – Glory!*

(Ref A.2)

Daddy's Waiting On You...

The Voyage Of Israel

THE PROMISE LAND
(Num. 13:26-27)

Milk, Honey & Grapes
Rest

THE WILDERNESS
(Deut. 8:2-3)

Quail, Manna, Water
Glory Cloud
Supernatural Interventions

Doubt, Unbelief, Complaint, Past
Place of Conflict

EGYPT
(Ex. 2:23-25)

Place of Bondage

Birth of Relationship

God Talks with Moses

A.2

THE CHRISTIAN WALK FROM BABYHOOD – TO ADOLESCENCE – TO MATURATION IN CHRIST

Prayerfully, by now you all have followed me through the process of the tabernacle of Moses and the voyage of Israel. They both are leading up to the last segment. As you may have already noticed, they all flow in a series of three. The same holds true of this one too. The difference is that we have become His tabernacle. We are His portable sanctuary. Every place we go we take God with us. Our temples (bodies) have become God's dwelling place.

As with the Outer Court and Egypt representing a place of bondage and rescue, every believer had to take that same walk. In our messed up degenerate state – while we were big and bad doing whatever we wanted to do when we wanted to do it, Christ died for us.

> *Romans 5:8*
> *But God commendeth his love toward us, in that, while we were yet sinners, Christ died for us.*
>
> *John 3:16*
> *For God so loved the world, that he gave his only begotten Son, that whosoever believeth in him should not perish, but have everlasting life.*

Romans 10:9
That If thou shalt confess with thy mouth the Lord Jesus, and shalt believe in thine heart that God hath raise him from the dead, thou shalt be saved.

As the sacrifice was slain on the Brazen Altar in the Outer Court, Christ was crucified on an old rugged cross outside of the city walls of Jerusalem. Every believer must accept the atoning work of Christ on that cross. From the cross of Christ at Calvary, Jesus died to do for us what we could never do for ourselves. It was in this state that God found Israel, and it's in this state that He found you and me. Here begins the birthing of our relationship.

Psalms 40:1-3
1. I waited patiently for the Lord; and he inclined unto me, and heard my cry.
2. He brought me up also out of an horrible pit, out of the miry clay, and set my feet upon a rock, and established my goings.
3. And he hath put a new song in my mouth, even praise unto our God: many shall see it, and fear, and shall trust in the Lord.

In the Outer Court, there was also the Laver. As believers, we, too, must take our wash. And I'm not talking about in mere water, but in the blood of Christ. The hymnist wrote, "What can wash away my sins? What can make me whole again? Nothing but the blood of Jesus."

Hebrews 9:12-14
12. Neither by the blood of goats and calves, <u>but by his own blood he entered in once into the holy place, having obtained eternal redemption for us</u>.

> *13. For if the blood of bulls and of goats, and the ashes of an heifer sprinkling the unclean, sanctifieth to the purifying of the flesh:*
> *14. How much more shall the blood of Christ, who through the eternal Spirit offered himself without spot to God, purge your conscience from dead works to serve the living God?*

As I previously stated, in the Old Testament, the high priest took the blood of animals, which was only sufficient for one year's covering of the people's sin. That blood would temporarily appease the Father, but if something is dead and just covered, it won't be long before it starts to stink. This is why every year they would have to go through this same cycle. Jesus' blood, however, was so potentate that it washed and purged our sins – those past, those present and those to come. (Thank you Jesus!) It permanently appeased the Father and even purged our sin guilt consciences. Now we can serve God unhindered by our past mistakes. ***We do not have to worry about whether He's going to answer because when He sees us, He really sees His Son's blood and God cannot deny Himself.*** In the book of Isaiah, God proclaims through the prophet, *"I, even I, am he that blotteth out thy transgressions for mine own sake, and will not remember thy sins."* (Isaiah 43:25) Now if He doesn't remember them, then neither should we.

Now that you understand that, the Apostle Paul comes along and says,

> *Romans 12:1-2*
> *1. I beseech you therefore, brethren, by the mercies of God, that ye present your bodies a living*

sacrifice, holy, acceptable unto God, [which is] your reasonable service.
2. And be not conformed to this world: but be ye transformed by the renewing of your mind, that ye may prove what [is] that good, and acceptable, and perfect, will of God.

In other words, He made Himself a sacrifice for you, now it's time for you to become a sacrifice for Him. In the Old Testament, when a sacrifice was slain that was the end of it. But now God says, I no longer want just a dead sacrifice but I want something dead and alive at the same time. What a paradox. Sounds similar to other passages like, "whosoever looses his life shall find it" and "give and it shall be given unto thee." But God says I still want something I can use. In Galatians chapter 2 verse 20, Paul says, *"I am crucified with Christ: nevertheless I live; yet not I, but Christ liveth in me: and the life which I now live in the flesh I live by the faith of the Son of God, who loved me, and gave himself for me."* But how can He truly use us? God says I've taken care of your spirit, now you must transform your mind, but you're going to have to crucify your flesh. The message is "Don't Get Stuck In The Outer Court." Many believers are stuck right here. You see them occasionally on Sundays but that's it. They've been loosed but refuse to be lead. They've been liberated but desire to stay in their Egypt. They've been delivered but without destiny. They have no real zest or zeal for the things of God. As a matter of fact, they don't even like to hang around Christians too much. They are satisfied right where they are. You may hear an occasional line like; it doesn't take all of that! Well, it may not take all that for you, but baby, when I look back over my life and I begin to reminisce on where He's brought me from – I'm giving God all I've got and some more!

Now, to you reading this book, I know I'm not speaking of you. The mere fact that you have gotten this far in the book is indicative that your thirst has persuaded you that there has to be more to this thing than just getting saved. For you there is a call; a gravitating pull requesting your presence in the Holy Place. The relationship formed here will take place as it did with the Israelites in the wilderness. For you, it is a place of imperfection; a place of partiality; a place of great temptations; a place of pain and suffering; a place of great struggle between your flesh and your spirit. It is also a place where you begin to fall in love with Daddy. He allows you to take a peek at Him. He allows you to experience problems so that He can manifest Himself as a problem solver. He allows sickness and then proves Himself as your healer. Here's the bottom line – If you never had problems, how would you know He could solve them? If you have never been sick, how would you know Him as your healer? If you have never been down to your last, how would you know Him as one who makes a way out of no way. Your misery will qualify you for your miracle. As far as I can see, the purpose of the wilderness never changes. When you want to walk close to Him, although you may not like it, the wilderness is absolutely necessary. You see, the more He brings me through, the more glimpses I get of Him. In the process, I come through knowing Him just a little better than I knew Him before. I often tell my class that the greater the level, the greater the devil, but also the greater my God! As for the war between the flesh and the Spirit, the Apostle Paul addresses this pain-staking subject in Galatians 5:17.

Galatians 5:17
For the flesh lusteth against the Spirit, and the Spirit against the flesh: <u>and these are contrary the</u>

<u>one to the other</u>: *so that ye cannot do the things that ye would.*

And here's another prime example....

Romans 7:15-25

[15] For that which I do I allow not: for what I would, that do I not; but what I hate, that do I. [16] If then I do that which I would not, I consent unto the law that it is good. [17] Now then it is no more I that do it, but sin that dwelleth in me. [18] For I know that in me (that is, in my flesh,) dwelleth no good thing: for to will is present with me; but how to perform that which is good I find not. [19] For the good that I would I do not: but the evil which I would not, that I do. [20] Now if I do that I would not, it is no more I that do it, but sin that dwelleth in me. [21] I find then a law, that, when I would do good, evil is present with me. [22] For I delight in the law of God after the inward man: [23] But I see another law in my members, warring against the law of my mind, and bringing me into captivity to the law of sin which is in my members. [24] O wretched man that I am! who shall deliver me from the body of this death? [25] I thank God through Jesus Christ our Lord. So then with the mind I myself serve the law of God; but with the flesh the law of sin.

What a cataclysmic struggle the Apostle Paul found himself in. When he wanted to do what was right, there appeared to be an unchangeable law that evil would always be present with him. I don't mean to bombard you with so many scriptures but Cain found himself in a similar position in the book of Genesis chapter 4 verses six and seven. *"And the LORD said unto Cain, Why art thou wroth?* (Why are you so angry Cain that I accepted your brother Abel's offering and not yours?) *and why is thy countenance fallen?* (Why are you walking around looking so sad?) *If thou doest well, shalt thou not be accepted?* (Don't you know that if you do what's right in My sight I'll accept it too?) *and if thou doest not well,* <u>*sin lieth at the door*</u>... (And well, if you decide not to, I just want to let you know that the devil is anxiously waiting to take you out.)" You must understand that the flesh and the Spirit will never agree. They are in constant conflict with each other. On one side there's the Works of the Flesh, and on the other side there's the Fruit of the Spirit. This struggle is more realized in the wilderness state of your relationship. The flesh will continuously encourage you to accept the ways of the world reminding you of who you were. For the flesh, sex outside of marriage every now and then is ok because God knows that we are only human. Homosexual relationships are made valid because they believe that they were born with the tendencies. There's nothing wrong with telling people off when they get on your nerves. Others should understand that you inherited momma's attitude. Abortions are ok at two months because it's not really a baby yet. There's nothing wrong with playing the lottery since God does work in mysterious ways. What a travesty it would be if you were to follow the dictates of your flesh. The Holy Spirit however will constantly remind you not of who you were but of who you have become in Christ. Your spirit will agree with the word of God and begin to say things like – the word of God does say that He is the supplier of all of your need; it does say that any sex outside of marriage is wrong; it does say that God made them male and female – not two males or two females; it does say that if any man be in Christ he is a new creation - old things are past away and all things are become new; it does say that you can get angry, but you better make sure you don't sin. I hope by now you have gained the significance of feeding your spirit man the word of God. It's a brutal fight between the flesh and the Spirit. Paul says this thing is so bad until after I've gotten through boxing, beating and buffeting my body - I bring it under subjection. I force it to comply with the leading of the Holy Spirit. He says otherwise I could find myself being rejected of God. (I Corinthians 9:24-27; 2 Corinthians 5:17; Philippians 4:19; 1 Thessalonians 4:3; Ephesians 4:26)

(Ref A.3; Ref A.4)

Rickey E. Macklin

THE GAME – THE WAR – THE FIGHT

S<small>PIRIT</small>   (M<small>IND</small>)   F<small>LESH</small>

Fruit of the Spirit	Referee Vs	Works of the Flesh
Love, Joy, Peace, Longsuffering, Gentleness, Goodness, Faith, Meekness & Temperance		Adultery, Fornication, Uncleanness, Lasciviousness, Idolatry, Witchcraft, Hatred, Variance, Emulations, Wrath, Strife, Seditions, Heresies, Envyings, murders, Drunkenness & Revellings
The Word of God		

Ref A.3

Daddy's Waiting On You...

FRUIT-CHECK

Works of the Flesh & Fruit of the Spirit

Works of the Flesh	Fruit of the Spirit
Adultery - Covenant Breakers and Immorality	**Love** - Strong affection; selfless act w/out condition; This affection is directed even toward unlovable!
Fornication - Two loves and Sexual Impurity	
Heresies – False doctrine that creates dissention in the faith	**Joy** – Gladness of Heart, Inward stability that God, through Jesus Christ, fortified by the Holy Ghost, on our behalf, has already worked the situation out!
Uncleanness – Indecency and Morally impure; filthy	
Lasciviousness – Excess, Greed, and Debauchery; over indulgence (sin)	**Peace** – Mildness combined with tenderness, quiet spirit; to be still, harmonious relationships
Idolatry – The worship of other gods i.e., people and things	
Witchcraft – Practices of witch; sorcery; magic. Evil spiritual influences	**Longsuffering** – long endurance with patience; forbearance "putting up with". It is the opposite of anger, and is associated with mercy
Hatred – Intense dislike or extreme hostility	
Variance – Shifty, indecisive, up & down Unstable – Double-minded	**Gentleness** – Not severe, rough, or violent but mild. Clement, Peaceful, Soothing, and Tender. The absence of bad temper and belligerence.
Emulations – Effort or desire to equal or excel others; competition	
Wrath – Strong stern, or fierce anger; Vengeance or punishment as a result	**Goodness** – Kindness, generosity, honorable, pleasant. Not merely goodness as a quality, rather it is goodness in action; is expressed in deeds.
Strife – Bitter conflict; quarrelsome; disagreement, opposition	
Seditions – discontentment or rebellion against authority; insurrection, mutiny	**Faith** – (Faithfulness) Can be trusted, and reliable (Especially with the things of God's)
Envyings – Desire what another has; covetous of their success or possessions	**Meekness** – Forbearing, yielding, humble heart, patient; Submissive spirit; Temper of spirit to accept without dispute the will of God
Murders – Killing of another human, also plans, ambition, and goals	
Drunkenness – Intoxication as with alcohol	**Temperance** - Self restraint in action, self control following knowledge of the word of God
Revellings – To rebel; make noise and take great pleasure in it.	

A.4

So, as I previously stated, the wilderness is indeed necessary. It was necessary for the Israelites to qualify for Canaan. It was necessary for Jesus to qualify for His anointing. And it is necessary for you and I to walk into God's next level of anointing. With the Israelites, an entire generation flunk the wilderness test.

> *Numbers 32:13*
> *13. And the Lord's anger was kindled against Israel, and he made them wander in the wilderness forty years, until all the generation, that had done evil in the sight of the Lord, was consumed.*

Jesus passed the wilderness test with flying colors and received power to walk into His destiny.

> *Luke 4:13,14*
> *13. And when the devil had ended all the temptation, he departed from him for a season.*
> *14. And Jesus returned in the power of the Spirit into Galilee...*

What about you dear one? Will there be pain? More than likely there will. Will there be disappointments? Yes! Are you going to have to endure some suffering? You may. Will people talk about you? They talked about Jesus. Will you be persecuted for righteousness sake? The servant is not greater than his Lord. If they persecuted Him, they will persecute you also. Will the doctor walk away and shake his head? He may. Will people count you out? I'm sure they will. Will you feel like giving up and throwing in the towel? Regardless of how spiritual you are, there will come a time in your life when you reach this point

– But God! I heard one preacher say, if you ever feel that you are at the end of your rope just tie a knot and hold on. Will you feel like God has forsaken you? You may. Oh, I'm sure you know the word and can probably quote more scriptures than me – but what do you do when it seems that God is no longer speaking to you? Everyone else has gotten a word of prophecy. Everyone else is getting cup over flowing blessings but you're being stripped of what you do have. Before you get all uptight and began to murmur and complain, know that God knows what He is doing. He knows how much you can handle. He made you and understands very well your breaking point. Isaiah prophetically speaking said, *"For my thoughts are not your thoughts, neither are your ways my ways, saith the Lord. For as the heavens are higher than the earth, so are my ways higher than your ways, and my thoughts than your thoughts."* (Isaiah 55:8,9) What are you saying Isaiah? It may seem that you're going down but you're coming up again. God says I have a plan to prosper you and not harm you. If I have to break you to make you, then I will. Your depth *will* determine your height and that's why I have to take you deep. But know that it's for my glory. So, don't try to figure this one out just trust Me. I need to work some things out of you and My fire is necessary.

HE SAYS YOUR DEPTH WILL DERTIMINE YOUR HEIGHT AND THAT'S WHY I HAVE TO TAKE YOU DEEP.

While you're going through your wilderness just grab a hold to these two promises of Mine. All things are working together for your good because you love Me and I've called You for My purpose. (Romans 8:28) And I won't allow any temptation to come your way that is not common or that others have not experienced. Know that I, God, Am faithful to My promise. I will not allow you to be tempted beyond your ability to come out victorious. When the devil brings the temptation, I will along with it provide you a way out or a way to keep you from falling. (1 Corinthians 10:13) What am I doing in the process? Well, after you've gone through; after you've suffered a while; after you've endured the hurt and the pain - I'm going to make you perfect (clean up all your faults and issues). I'm going to establish you (solidify your position in Me and remove all your doubts). I'm going to settle you (like cement, you'll be unmoved by everything but Me). (1 Peter 5:10)

So, as you can see, the wilderness of your relationship will be a season of temptations and struggles, but God will see you through it. However, I don't believe anyone purposely wants to be in a place like this for the rest of his or her life. With the Israelites, an entire generation died here never having experienced the promise. What about you? Will you die in your wilderness? Will you settle here or is there something inside you saying, "More! More! There has to be more." Are you satisfied or is there yet inside of your belly a deep calling? An *Outer Court relationship* was all right at first and the *Inner Court relationship* was even better, but now how about a relationship in the *Most Holy Place*? Can you not hear the voice of Daddy saying come closer my son – come closer my daughter? He's calling you to a beyond the vail relationship.

As you slip beyond the vail, in the splendor of His glory as with the angels in the book of Isaiah chapter six and in Revelation chapter four, all you can do is cry – Holy! Holy! Holy! The weight of His glory drives you to your knees to worship Him. And in the light of His perfection, you begin to see how imperfect you really are. My God! All of your talents, your accolades, your degrees, your credentials, and your status mean nothing!

THE WEIGHT OF HIS GLORY DRIVES YOU TO YOUR KNEES TO WORSHIP HIM.

Daddy is not looking to be entertained. He wants you – all of you. Can't you hear Him calling you? Come closer my son, Come closer my daughter. But the closer you get, the filthier you look because the pure light of God illuminates all the dark areas in your life. Dirty heart, nasty attitude, bitterness, envy, and jealousy – and just think … you would never know if you weren't allowed this access into His presence. You almost want to question Him and ask, are you really talking to me Daddy? But He says, Come closer. How is it that a Holy God would allow me into His presence? Does He love me that much? Somehow, you know that the answer is yes. What a place to be! When you get to this point, you no longer operate by the law but rather by love. This is not simply a religious experience. Here's what I'm saying. If you're driving down the highway doing 65 miles an hour but the speed limit is 55 when you see a cop – what do you do? Yes, you slow down. But why? You do it to avoid getting a traffic ticket. You obey because you don't want to pay the price for not obeying. That's legalism! Life is full of decisions and every decision carries a consequence. But on the other hand, when love is introduced into the picture, the entire scenario changes. For instance, in the Outer Court you obeyed Him because you were afraid {Legalism}. In the Inner Court, it was a combination of fear and love {Religion}, but in the Most Holy Place it's absolute love {Relationship}. What are you talking about, Minister Rickey? Keep reading and I'll tell you. You know that you have grown to a point of matured love when you are no longer legalistic in your relationship. You obey God not because you are afraid of going to hell but because you love Him and don't want to disappoint Him. In other words, while the law restricts you, love, on the other hand, constrains you. Your greatest desire is to keep a smile on Daddy's face.

What is so unique about this Most Holy Place relationship? Well, it's a place of sweatless victories; a place where His strength is made perfect in your weakness; a place where you exist in the peace of God that transcends human understanding; a place where you exist in the finished works of Christ; a place of no worries; a place of total reliance and absolute trust in Him; a place where exclusively the Holy Spirit leads you. In this place, if God doesn't say move, you'll stay where you are. If He doesn't say speak, you'll refuse to open up your mouth and conjure up something you think He may have said. In this place, you know that your times are in His hands (Psalms 31:15). And then He says to you, I've been waiting on you for such a long time. There's so much I have wanted to tell you. I have the answers to all of your questions. Let's go to the other side of the mountain – just you and me. Let's just bask in the lilies of the field. Listen for a moment and let Me speak. All of your pain, hurts, and disappointments, I felt them too. As for your tears, how can I forget each one that rolled down your face? The first step you took as a child; the first time you rode a bike without falling; perhaps your earthly daddy wasn't there, but I was. Whether skating, riding a bike, winning a beauty contest, or a football game, Daddy was there either on the sideline or in the audience. How could I have missed those precious moments? The first time you fell in love; the first time someone broke your heart; when love ones left you willingly and sometimes not so willingly, I was there. I speak now not to your shame or to invade your privacy, but every struggle that you've had and that you still have, I know about them. Shhhhhhhhh... I know it's a secret and you don't want anyone else to know, but I love you in spite of it. That's why I sent my Spirit. He'll keep you from falling. The truth of the matter is before I ever placed you in your mother's womb, you were on My mind. My love for you is beyond your human capacity to comprehend. Wow! And this is just the beginning of the conversation between you and Daddy. (Jeremiah 1:4-10); (Psalms 139:14-18); (Jude 1:24)

In the Old Testament, only the high priest could enter in, take care of business and get out. But now we have the awesome invitation and privilege of entering and just hanging out with Daddy as long as we like. He wants us to hang around until we develop His heartbeat. My statement to you is after you have developed this type of relationship with Him, how dare you settle for, reconnect with or waste your time on something in the Outer Court/Egypt when He has brought you into your land of promise. (Ref A.5)

Rickey E. Macklin

The Christian Today

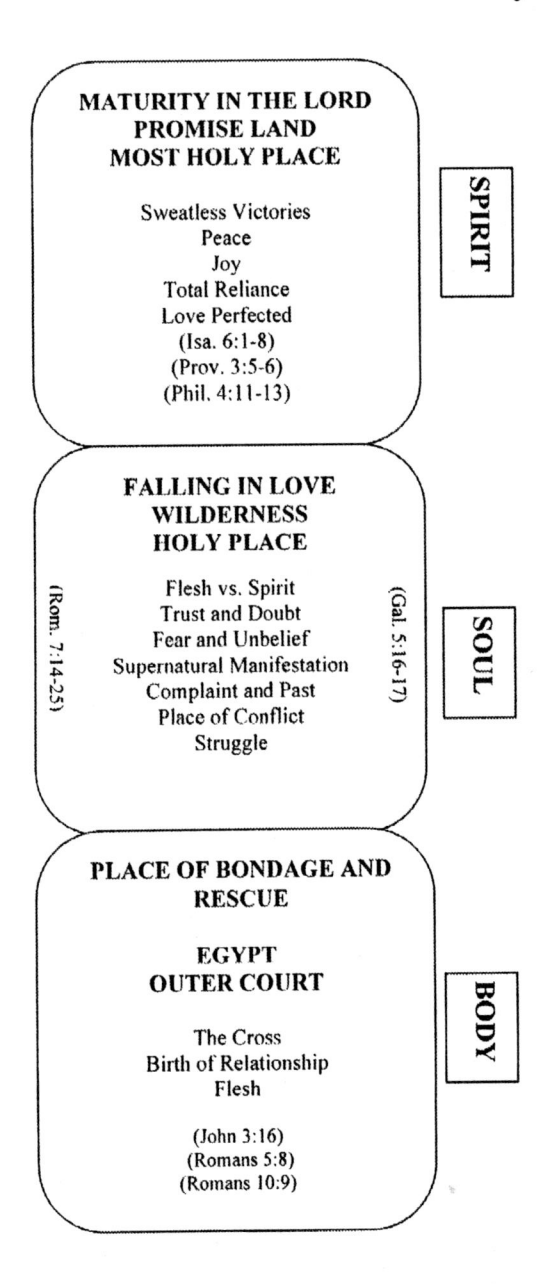

**MATURITY IN THE LORD
PROMISE LAND
MOST HOLY PLACE**

Sweatless Victories
Peace
Joy
Total Reliance
Love Perfected
(Isa. 6:1-8)
(Prov. 3:5-6)
(Phil. 4:11-13)

SPIRIT

**FALLING IN LOVE
WILDERNESS
HOLY PLACE**

Flesh vs. Spirit
Trust and Doubt
Fear and Unbelief
Supernatural Manifestation
Complaint and Past
Place of Conflict
Struggle

(Rom. 7:14-25) (Gal. 5:16-17)

SOUL

PLACE OF BONDAGE AND RESCUE

**EGYPT
OUTER COURT**

The Cross
Birth of Relationship
Flesh

(John 3:16)
(Romans 5:8)
(Romans 10:9)

BODY

A.5

CHAPTER FIVE
SHOW ME YOUR GLORY

Rickey E. Macklin

SHOW ME YOUR GLORY

In Exodus 33 verses 18 and 20 Moses said, *"I beseech thee, shew me thy glory."* God spoke to Moses and said, *"Thou canst not see my face: for there shall no man see me, and live."* Moses' desire was to experience the manifold and manifested expression of God Himself. What was the price tag attached to this kind of expression? God said everyone who desires this expression must first die. In other words Moses, *only dead men see my face.* But Moses was willing to pay the price. Do you really want to see His glory? Do you really want to see His face?

Exactly what could Moses have been speaking of when he requested of God to see His glory? In response to his request, in verses twenty-two and twenty-three God said to Moses, *"And it shall come to pass, while **my glory passeth by**, that I will put thee in a clift of the rock, and will cover thee with my hand while I pass by: And I will take away mine hand, and thou shalt see my back parts: but my face shall not be seen."* The Hebrew word for glory is *kabod* and the Greek word is *doxa*. Kabod means to be heavy (weighty) i.e., wealth, honor, dignity and power. Doxa means reputation, fame, splendor and majesty. The glory of God is an expression of His uniqueness. It distinguishes Him from all that He has created. It means honor or excellent reputation – the visible manifestation of the excellence of God's character. It's an expression of His perfect holiness and His detachment from the world, but also His deliberate intention to reveal Himself to mankind. A good example of this duality of God is seen within the tabernacle. If you recall from the last chapter, there was a vail that separated the holy of holies from the holy place. On the one side of it was contact with the indescribable glory of the most holy God and on the other side with the desperate need of sinful mankind. Outside trapped – not ever coming to know whom He really is. You see, until you make that voyage beyond the vail, you'll never really know Him either.

ON THE ONE SIDE OF IT WAS CONTACT WITH THE INDESCRIBABLE GLORY OF THE MOST HOLY GOD
AND ON THE OTHER SIDE WITH THE DESPERATE NEED OF SINFUL MANKIND

So, again what was Moses really saying? In essence, God give me a greater revelation of who you really are. Nothing could satisfy him more and nothing should satisfy us more than a greater revelation of Him. When God's glory passed by Moses, he experienced all of God's goodness. In the Old Testament, however, they beheld the glory but in the New Testament we reflect it. Look at it this way. The moon as beautiful and bright as it appears on a nice clear night has no light in and of itself. It reflects the light of the sun. As for you and I, when we draw nigh unto Daddy and we receive His Spirit, not only do we get a greater revelation of Him, but also begin to reflect His character traits like holiness, love, mercy, goodness, kindness and longsuffering. I believe you got the point. Can't you see the need now for His glory? But you're not going to experience His glory in sin. As with Isaiah, after King Uzziah died he received a revelation of God. With that revelation, the prophet Isaiah saw how filthy, unclean and messed up he was. It wasn't until the coal touched his lips and purging took place that he received the greater revelation. It was at this point that Isaiah could truly represent God. He said, here I am – send me! This is where I believe lots of people get stuck. They build ministries off of just a revelation and start businesses off of just a revelation and get marriage off of just a revelation. They've made it beyond the vail but haven't hung around long enough. They've felt His presence but have not yet seen His face. I don't know about you but I need a greater revelation. Now, since you've made it this far, why don't you pull your coat off; loosen your tie; kick your shoes off; lay prostrate before Him and get your greater revelation. I don't want to simply get a glance of Daddy. I want to look like Him! Show Me Your Glory! Before you go any further, cry out to Him and say Daddy, show me your glory!

CHAPTER SIX

MAINTAINING INTIMACY WITH DADDY

MAINTAINING INTIMACY

After developing this kind of relationship, you would assume that the rest of your life would be as a bed of roses, right? Not so. The word of God says that Christ is washing us with the water of the word that one day we will be presented as a bride without spot or wrinkle. (Ephesians 5:25-27) The truth of the matter is we are being perfected and as of now, none of us has arrived at our final destination.

> *Romans 8:29*
> *For whom he did foreknow, he also did predestinate to be conformed to the image of his Son, that he might be the firstborn among many brethren.*

Our prayer is to one day look like little Jesus' walking around. Therefore, even after hanging out with Daddy there is still a tendency to slip back and forth into the Holy Place/Inner Court relationship. One season we give Him our all, and the next season when problems arise, we act as if He needs our help.

So, how do we get His attention and how do we maintain it? First of all, the only thing that truly impresses Him is when you give Him your whole heart. At the beginning, we pledged to Him our whole heart and we gave it to Him. However, because of His goodness and mercy, we sometimes have a tendency to take Him for granted. We become distracted by the gifts and lose sight of the Giver. Our affections shift from the Creator to the created. Our convictions change and things that bothered us so much at first have very little affect, if any. Why? Because the further we are away from Him the less convictions we experience. If you recall in the previous chapter, it was His light that illuminated the dark areas in our lives that enabled us to cast them aside. But how do you drift to this point when you were so close to Him? The answer is a progressive loss of intimacy. And where there is a progressive loss of intimacy, there is a breakdown in communion and communication. Let me put it this way for the married men. Would your wife happily give you all your heart desires if you haven't given her any love, affection or attention in the past six months? No! No love, no affection, no attention, no communion, no communication, no intimacy…no into me – you see! The devil's plan has not changed. He still desires to kill, steal and destroy your relationship. More importantly, if you recall in my last book, *God's Whole Armor*, the enemy is especially jealous of the relationship that we have with God because we have taken His place.

Excerpt from "God's Whole Armor" (pg 27)
"Jesus made it plain, when He said, the enemy really doesn't hate you per se, he hates who and what you stand for. Understand something – you are first on God's agenda; you are the apple of His eye (Psalms 17:8) and as such, why wouldn't an ole' dirty, stinking, low down, snagged tooth, cowardly devil try to inflict pain on you and kill that which is most important to God?"

He will, therefore, come up with every trick possible and distraction to pull us out of Daddy's presence.

Secondly, we maintain with this principle in mind. "Whatever it takes to get a person it takes to keep them." In the natural, it's very easy for us to understand this concept. For instance, when men find themselves interested in women, they do whatever it takes to win their affections. In some cases, they'll do it for years. However, once they've won the heart of the women, they have a tendency to fall short of some of those same things they initially did to win them. The flowers cease to come in. Words of affection now come once in a blue moon and gifts are only exchanged during special occasions, if the occasions are even remembered. I believe that if you are courting before marriage, there's no reason why you shouldn't court after marriage. As a matter of fact, just court for the rest of your lives. You see, we, too, are courting. We are courting His Son.

Here are several things I find necessary to maintain spiritual intimacy with Him.

- Continue to study His word (2 Timothy 2:15)
    - To maintain spiritual intimacy, each believer must make it his or her quest to become a lifetime student of the word of God. Dr. Myles Munroe once stated, *"All that you know is all that you have learned but all that you have learned is not all there is to know."*

- Continue to meditate on Him and His promises throughout the day (Joshua 1:8)
    - To maintain spiritual intimacy, the believer must learn to meditate on Daddy and His promises. You will notice at the end of the day that there was not much time left to meditate on anything else.

- Continue to set aside a specific time for just you and Him on a daily basis (Psalms 63:1)
    - To maintain spiritual intimacy, the believer must allot time on a daily basis to invest with Daddy. With this time, you will increase your fellowship, communion and intimacy with Him.

- Invest more time with the Holy Spirit – seek His guidance (John 16:13)
    - To maintain spiritual intimacy, the believer must invest time with the Holy Spirit. He has the answers to your desires and needs. Jesus said to the disciples upon His transition that the Holy Spirit would come after Him. It's good that you've invested time getting to know Jesus but now do not be found guilty of grieving He the Holy Spirit.

- Pray continuously (1 Thessalonians 5:17)
    - To maintain spiritual intimacy, the believer must be prayerful at all times. Whenever there are issues of concern, we can always receive the answers we need in prayer.

- Talk to Him throughout the day (Deuteronomy 5:24; John 16:13)
    - To maintain spiritual intimacy, the believer must talk to God daily. God is talking. The question is are you listening? Talk to Him on your job sitting at your computer,

riding in your car, or standing at the bus stop. He's waiting. Oh, don't forget to listen to hear what He has to say.

- Continue to praise & worship Him daily (Psalms 34:1; John 4:23,24)
  - To maintain spiritual intimacy, the believer must develop a lifestyle of praise and worship. The atmosphere that is created will cause God to dwell with you and not just pay frequent visits.

- Make more investments in your library with material for your spiritual growth and less for entertainment (Psalms 119:11,38,105,140)
  - To maintain spiritual intimacy, the believer must make this investment. The Holy Spirit will lead you to the right material. At some point, your religious library should excel your secular. God's word will offer you wisdom that worldly magazines could never.

- Add fasting to your agenda (Mark 9,28,29; Luke 2: 37,38; 2 Corinthians 6:4-10)
  - To maintain spiritual intimacy, the believer must develop a lifestyle of fasting. As I stated previously, this will aid you tremendously in keeping your flesh in subjection.

If you are going to maintain, you are going to have to give Him your devotion. You must be consumed with Him and Him only. If He cannot be number one, He will not be number two. And sometimes in being close to Him, mandates are placed upon your life that may never be requested of others.

IF HE CANNOT BE NUMBER ONE, HE WILL NOT BE NUMBER TWO.

Take a quick look at this passage given by Jesus Himself and draw your own conclusion.

> *Luke 9:59-62*
> *59. And he said unto another, Follow me. But he said, Lord, suffer me first to go and bury my father.*
> *60. Jesus said unto him, Let the dead bury their dead: but go thou and preach the kingdom of God.*
> *61. And another also said, Lord, I will follow thee; but let me first go bid them farewell, which are at home at my house.*
> *62. And Jesus said unto him, No man, having put his hand to the plough, and looking back, is fit for the kingdom of God.*

These are signs to us that yes, Daddy loves us and want affectionately to invest time with us and use us. But He's not looking for a half-hearted saint. He's not looking for a part-time lover. We wouldn't want to be anyone's part-time lover, just as God doesn't want to be ours. We want all of someone and God wants all of us. He's not interested in a girlfriend. He's looking for someone who's ready to make a lifetime commitment. Since Daddy wants to talk to us and has so much He wants to say, why not give Him His due time and develop an ear to hear what He has to say?

Daddy's Waiting On You...

CONCLUSION
COME CLOSER...

CONCLUSION

So, what's the crux of this entire book? Daddy has sent out an invitation to you. He wants you to meet Him "beyond the vail." In Matthew 13:8, Jesus speaks of the word as producing three folds of harvest. *"But other fell into good ground, and brought forth fruit, some an hundredfold, some sixtyfold, some thirtyfold."* I believe the correlation of these three folds and the three realms we discussed in the book are very clear. The hundredfold is reserved for those who desperately desire to make their dwelling place the Holy of Holies. It is here that they become as He is. The sixtyfold is reserved for those who have been filled with the Spirit but refuse to be led beyond the Holy Place. The thirtyfold unfortunately is reserved for those that are determined to remain babes in the Outer Court. Is a thirtyfold harvest all that you want? Aren't you tired of just going to church, just being churched? Aren't you tired of simply going through the motions? I can appreciate the fact that the God I serve has no equal, but if I cannot connect with Him, what good is it? From day to day, I experience some things that sometimes I can't tell anybody, but it really does my heart good to know that I can go to Him and He hears me and answers me.

Now, Daddy's calling you. He is calling you to a place in Him where He constantly manifests Himself; a place in Him where there is divine revelation; a place in Him where you develop His heartbeat; a place where there are answers to all of your questions. Has your thirst not overwhelmed you and your hunger consumed you? A thirst that no created thing could quench and a hunger that your earthly appetite has failed to satisfy. If so, there is a place right next to Daddy. Do you remember David's pursuit of this place in Psalms 27:4? *He stated that there was only one thing that he desired of the Lord* (one desire that was the sum of them all) *and that he would seek* (search and pursue) *after; that he may dwell* (inhabit, occupy, abide, live, reside, stay*) in the house of the Lord all the days of his life.* To do what? *To behold the beauty of the Lord.* God's beauty is that attribute of God whereby He is the sum of everything desirable and far exceeds all other desires. And what else was on David's mind? *To inquire in His temple.* I have a lot of unanswered questions that I know can only be answered in the glory. David went on to say in Psalms 73:25, *"Whom have I in heaven but thee? and there is none upon earth that I desire beside thee."* Now, tell me, shouldn't you have this same desire? Shouldn't you have this same pursuit? At some point in the process, you will discover that the pursuer will have become the pursued. God will overtake you and you will have become His dwelling place – *His tabernacle.* If you really want to know life's answers, then accept God's call. He's waiting… Can't you hear Him? He's calling you. Come closer.

SCRIPTURES TO ASSIST YOU IN YOUR JOURNEY BEYOND THE VAIL

Ephesians 2:13,14
13. But now in Christ Jesus ye who sometimes were far off are made nigh by the blood of Christ.
14. For he is our peace, who hath made both one, and hath broken down the middle wall of partition between us;

Psalms 63:1
1. O God, thou art my God; early will I seek thee: my soul thirsteth for thee, my flesh longeth for thee in a dry and thirsty land, where no water is;

1 Chronicles 16:10-11
10. Glory ye in his holy name: let the heart of them rejoice that seek the Lord.
11. Seek the Lord and his strength, seek his face continually.

I Chronicles 22:19
19. Now set your heart and your soul to seek the Lord your God; arise therefore, and build ye the sanctuary of the Lord God, to bring the ark of the covenant of the Lord, and the holy vessels of God, into the house that is to be built to the name of the Lord.

2 Chronicles 15:12
12. And they entered into a covenant to seek the Lord God of their fathers with all their heart and with all their soul;

Psalms 34:10,15,18
10. The young lions do lack, and suffer hunger: but they that seek the Lord shall not want any good thing.
15. The eyes of the Lord are upon the righteous, and his ears are open unto their cry.
18. The Lord is nigh unto them that are of a broken heart; and saveth such as be of a contrite spirit.

Psalms 105:1-4
1. O Give thanks unto the Lord; call upon his name: make known his deeds among the people.
2. Sing unto him, sing psalms unto him: talk ye of all his wondrous works.
3. Glory ye in his holy name: let the heart of them rejoice that seek the Lord.
4. Seek the Lord, and his strength: seek his face evermore.

Proverbs 28:5
5. Evil men understand not judgment: but they that seek the Lord understand all things.

Hosea 10:13
13. Sow to yourselves in righteousness, reap in mercy; break up your fallow ground: for it is time to

seek the Lord, till he come and rain righteousness upon you.

Acts 17:27
27. That they should seek the Lord, if haply they might feel after him, and find him, though he be not far from every one of us:

Isaiah 55:6-7
6. Seek ye the Lord while he may be found, call ye upon him while he is near:
7. Let the wicked forsake his way, and the unrighteous man his thoughts: and let him return unto the Lord, and he will have mercy upon him; and to our God, for he will abundantly pardon.

Matthew 5:6
6. Blessed are they which do hunger and thirst after righteousness: for they shall be filled.

REFERENCES

Scriptures are used from the Authorized King James Version Bible.

Erickson, Millard J., *Christian Theology*. Second Edition, Baker Books, 1998

Grudem, Wayne, *Systematic Theology*. Zondervan Publishing House, 1994

Macklin, Rickey, *God's Whole Armor*. First Books Library, 2001

Tenney, Tommy, *God Chasers*. Destiny Image, 1999

Webster's Encyclopedic Unabridged Dictionary of the English Language. Gramercy Books, 1994

Webster's II New Revised University Dictionary. Riverside Publishing Company, 1984

OTHER BOOK BY AUTHOR

God's Whole Armor

Minister Rickey E. Macklin, Author

$14.00

For those of you who have been eagerly anticipating arrival of this new book "God's Whole Armor," it has finally been released from the press. Minister Macklin, through his own struggles discovered a simple solution to why we, as children of the Most High God, continue to fall prey to the tricks of the devil. This inspired masterpiece outlines in detail who your enemy is and his modus operendi. Minister Macklin then gives detailed instructions on how to put on and activate each part of the armor of God that enables you to:

"STAND AGAINST THE WILES OF THE DEVIL!"

THIS BOOK IS GUARANTEED TO CHANGE YOUR LIFE!
www.ambassador4christ.org

For information, contact:
Ambassadors for Christ
P.O. Box 263
Temple Hills, MD 20757
C/O Rickey E. Macklin

http://www.ambassador4christ.org
ministeric@ambassador4christ.org

ABOUT THE AUTHOR

Minister Rickey E. Macklin, son of Reverend and Mrs. Arthur Macklin Sr. of Camden, S.C., is a graduate of South Carolina State University and Jericho Christian Training College, and has his Master's in Theology from National Bible Seminary. Minister Macklin is President/CEO of Ambassadors For Christ Ministries where the ministry's primary purpose is to provide books, bible studies and various resources to assist Christians in discovering their God-given purposes. Minister Macklin is co-leader of the Jericho Singles Ministry, and serves as leader of The Mighty Men of Valor. He teaches "Christian Courtship" at the Jericho Christian Training College and has produced a book to supplement the course. He is the author of the Spirit-filled masterpiece "God's Whole Armor."

Printed in the United States
45175LVS00002B/313-330